# Fugitives

# Fugitives

*Donald Campbell*

Grace Note
Publications

*Fugitives*
This edition published 2015 by
Grace Note Publications C.I.C.
Grange of Locherlour,
Ochtertyre, PH7 4JS,
Scotland

books@gracenotereading.co.uk
www.gracenotepublications.co.uk

ISBN 978-1-907676-72-7

Cover designed by Grace Note Publications.

As always, for Jean

# Contents

## NEW POEMS

# UNCOLLECTED POEMS

## The Wonderful World of Ned Holt

## To Poets

## Thinking of Norman MacCaig

## And More ...

# TRANSLATIONS

## Poems from the Native American Nations

## Other Translations

## Notes on the Poems      119

## About the Poet      125

# Fugitives

The poems collected here fall into three categories; these are new poems, previously uncollected poems, and translations. Most of them have appeared at one time or another in the following magazines; *Akros, Chapman, Fras, Gallimaufry, Glasgow Review, Lines Review, South Bank Review* **and** *Scotia Review.* Several have been broadcast and one, Ballade for Poethon 91, was specially commissioned by *The Guardian* newspaper. I should also acknowledge Edinburgh Central Library, who first published my Ned Holt poems on their Capital Collections website. In addition, I have performed these poems at readings all over Scotland, occasionally in England and, on one memorable occasion, in Wales.

Over the years, a definite change in style has occurred in my verse. Until the publication of my *Selected Poems* in 1990, all my poetry was written in Scots, primarily for the sake of performance. I was taking part in poetry readings more or less continually and it seemed perfectly reasonable to ensure that the printed text reflected the poems as they were spoken. Recently, however, I have become much more interested in the way the poems *look* on the printed page. My interest in traditional forms has led – for some reason that I do not fully understand – to most of my recent work employing Standard English.

I have not deserted the Scots language completely, however. While it may be true that I am less committed to the Lowland Scots Tradition than I used to be, Scots was my first language, the language of my background and remains a language that I still use in certain circumstances. In my poems, I continue to make use of Scots words and idioms whenever they are appropriate.

*Donald Campbell, 2015*

# A note on influences, tastes and methods

I started writing poetry when I still in my teens, in much the same spirit as other boys took to football or pop music. This interest began at school although not, as one might expect, in the classroom. At that age, I was considered troublesome by my teachers and was often obliged to spend frequent periods of detention in the school library. This is where I discovered the poets who were to be my first influences; Dylan Thomas, Hugh MacDiarmid, Norman MacCaig, Maurice Lindsay, Sydney Tremayne, Alexander Scott, George Bruce and Robert Garioch. These poets are still important to me and I still read them every now and then. Later on, I became interested in the work of my own generation – Alan Bold, Alistair Mackie, Duncan Glen, Tom Leonard, Walter Perrie, Valerie Gillies and Liz Lochhead. Through my work as a Writer-in-Residence, I came in contact with even younger poets – Kathleen Jamie, George Gunn, Ron Butlin and Catherine Czerkawska – and I still read their work whenever I come across it.

Most of these writers are Scots, of course, but I enjoy the work of English, Welsh Irish and American poets too; Roger McGough, Adrian Henri, Tom Paulin, Seamus Heaney, Simon Armitage and – most of all –

Charles Causley and Wendy Cope. I have read them all at one time or another and, although I cannot say I have felt any particular influence from any of them, one never can tell about these things. Although I don't review poetry as much as I once did, I remain interested enough to take a look at anything new that comes my way. I subscribe to a number of magazines – *Fras*, *South Bank Review* etc. – and while I agree with Stephen Fry's statement that 'much poetry written today suffers from anaemia' I am often surprised and delighted by what I read.

As far as my own practice is concerned, I am essentially a lyric poet – besides my poetry, I have also written songs for my plays – and I have an abiding interest in the relationship between form and content. For a number of reasons, I tend to employ set forms; they are interesting to write; the tension between form and content creates an intensity of utterance that seems missing when I try to write free verse; lastly, I believe that the use of a set form expands and enhances the meaning of the poem.

*Donald Campbell, 2015*

# New Poems

Most of these poems focus on the city in which I have spent most of my life and the people who have been most important to me. The exceptions are those poems which relate to my childhood in Caithness.

## Chateau en Ecosse

Edwin's castle, in its height
bathed above us in floodlight
shines serenely in the night.

Dark Age stronghold, royal seat,
looming over Princes Street,
Our signature image, last retreat.

Steadfast, solid, strong and true,
its weaknesses are very few.
Upon this rock our city grew.

The presence of such passive might
like a beacon burning bright
fills us with pride and much delight.

## Rutland Square

*Walking today in Rutland Square*
*I visited my memories there;*
*A taxi standing in the rain;*
*The smoke of a departing train.*
*Suddenly, it seemed quite clear.*
*My childhood whispered in my ear.*

Walking today in Rutland Square
My mother's face was everywhere.
And it gave me such a thrill
to find her presence with me still
today as I walked in Rutland Square.

I visited my memories there,
Like Frankie Laine and Johnny Ray,
Debbie Reynolds, Doris Day.
Ginger Rogers, Fred Astaire
might dance all night in Rutland Square.

A taxi standing in the rain;
I blinked three times and saw it plain.
Just like the one that used to come
to pick me up and take me home.
For years, I've looked for it in vain.

The smoke of an approaching train
is mere illusion now, I fear.
The Caley station's long been gone
and Waverley now serves alone.
There's now fresh air in Rutland Square.

Suddenly, it seemed quite clear!
The lack of style, absence of grace,
the faults so evident elsewhere
can find no home within this space.
The source of squalor and despair
can find no home in Rutland Square.

My childhood whispers in my ear,
reminding me of things held dear;
the corner where we used to meet;
the clang of trams in Princes Street;
St. George's, where the congregation prayed;
La Fiesta, where the music played

And all my secrets were laid bare,
As I walked today through Rutland Square,

## In St. Giles

Out of the chaos of the town
I come again to this sacred place
where history meets with faith and grace.

Seated here, all on my own,
My muse keeps striving for release
Out of the chaos of the town
I'm here again in this sacred space.

And as I slowly look around
my principles fall into place.
Such tranquillity I would embrace.
and fear to look on no man's face
as, out of the chaos of the town
I find myself in this sacred place.

## Scott Monument

Remember, it is no whited sepulchre,
this symbol of our land and race,
emblem of everything we have and are
centred capitally in its favoured place,
pointing so proudly into space;
structured in stone and shining grace,
standing over the station whose very name
came from the same, enduring flame.


Under the canopy, Carrara gleams.
Sir Walter in marble is quite at ease.
Overhead lurks the stuff of his dreams:
Dandy Dinmont, old Meg Merrilees.
Rob Roy hanging in the breeze
With Prince Charles Edward, if you please.
Baillie Nicol Jarvie, it would seem
lies buried beneath a cloud of steam.


The fires are all out – and now we dream.
Is it time for a brand-new age to dawn?
Can soot disperse, revealing Craigleith cream?
Can the carbon crust crack below the sun?
Can stonework shine again where once it shone?
Can so much damage ever be undone?
The black tower stands, whatever come may,
to service a debt we can never repay.

# Marchmont Morning

Sunlight on slate: our Castle's height
greets us with every day breaking;
rising from the sullen night
challenging us anew at waking.
Such a magnificent sight
that's always ours for the taking;
part of our flesh, part of our bone,
this is our history, set up in stone.


Well-drilled tenements on either hand
line the length and breadth of every street.
Straight as an arrow each of them was planned,
sharpening the corners where they meet.
Their appearance may not seem so grand
but Redhall sandstone's always hard to beat.
Flat over flat, landing on landing,
this is our heritage, solidly standing.


As Marchmont people leave their homes,
travelling to work or study or play,
the school bell rings, the postman comes
and so begins another day.
Students strutting with their chums,
prancing once more in fashionable array,
brighten the street, their colours adorning
the life that we lead on this brave Marchmont morning

## Bruntsfield Links

Early in the morning, when the world is still,
with putter and wedge I make my way
to Bruntsfield Links and try my skill
on eighteen holes of short-course play.

Practice may not make perfect but
so pleasantly it starts the day.
I swing and shoot and pitch and putt
and shank and hook and all the rest.

Sometimes I'm lucky with my shot
And sometimes not. I try my best
at every hole to match my par.
I sometimes get it right and pass the test.

Although I know I'll never be a star
And play the game for exercise and pleasure
I struggle every day to raise the bar,
Improve my game and take the measure

of this ancient course. The odd good score
plus a glut of memories to treasure;
To sink a putt, to see my tee-shots soar;
To pitch from rough into a rolling green;
That's all I want. What need for more?

In wintertime, I keep my interest keen;
a smaller course serves to suit my daily drill.
Nine holes may seem a trifle mean
yet it's enough for me to test my skill
early in the morning, when the world is still

## Portobello: Out of Season

It feels like March although it's May.
A wicked wind, an angry sea
disrupts this local holiday.

This is no place for you and me.
There's nowhere to go, nothing to see
We're out of season; out of reach
lie all the pleasures of the beach;

*No candyfloss, no fish and chips;*
*No donkey rides, no sailing trips.*

Nothing's still as we supposed;
such memories cannot be jolted.
All boarded up, barred and bolted,
the Portobello we knew is not disposed
to please us; it's quite definitely closed.

## The Water of Leith

This giggling girl, gurgling, gushing,
Trips into town, carefully brushing
Aside all the sights that like to ignore her.
Unruffled, unrushing, she sweeps all before her.

From Balerno and Baberton to Juniper Green
She slips along splendidly, sleek and serene
Passing Woodhall and Spylaw to Craiglockhart Dell
through Redhall and Roseburn to St. Bernard's Well.

The sun on her surface is gleaming and glittering.
The birds on her banks are ceaselessly twittering
High in the trees, where they huddle in hiding;
Chattering, chittering, as past she comes gliding.

She doesn't need rhyme, she doesn't need reason;
She wanders discretely, whatever the season.
Here's to her beauty, here's to her song!
Here's to the sight of her, strolling along!

# Springvalley

*Another Poem for Jean*

Last night I dreamed that once again
I made my way down Cuddy Lane,
returning home to Number Ten

Springvalley Terrace, where
I climbed that old familiar stair
and knew I'd find you waiting there,

where you used to sit with me
beside that copper canopy
that shines still in my memory.

My sweetest love, my dearest friend
upon this much you may depend;
from now until the utmost end

of all my days, I never will
forget the wonder and the thrill
of our first home – and still

I look up whenever we go by
at the windows, set on high
at our old building, and then I

**17**

remember oh, so very well
the friendly jingle of our bell,
the sight, the sound, the very smell

of that honest street we knew
when first I was in love with you
and you with me. We two

could never hope to thrive apart.
and at the end as at the start
I'll keep Springvalley in my heart.

# Reviewer

Smug as a stand-up, she
takes herself so seriously.
This sullen mediocrity
who loves to grouse
steps into the stalls for all to see
she's in the house.

She's high on ego, low on tact:
she cannot write, direct or act
yet her opinions stand as fact –
Oh, what a shocker!
The talents that, in youth, she lacked
return to mock her.

All the same, that's no excuse.
Her notices are so obtuse,
so full of malice and abuse
of all who heed them,
and are not really of much use
to those who read them.

# Wheeziana

*For George Gunn*

I guess by now he must be dead;
Old Banjo Ted, who used to come
to the front door of our old home.
The so-called banjo that he played
was like his music; quite home-made.
This was the only song he sung
quite tunelessly
with most of the words completely wrong.

*Oh, Wheeziana! Hev a cuppie tea!*
*I'll be coming for ye with a banjo on my knee!*

"No harm in him." The neighbours said.
"Poor soul, he's aye been soft in the head."
They laughed at him but loved him, too –
fixed him up with a old tool shed
where he stored his things and made his bed.
The only home he ever knew,
Ted used to call the place 'Sea View'

Such a life is simply led.
Dear Banjo Ted!
Can he really be dead?

## The Sound of the City

I learned to love this city for its sound.
In black-out years, when I was very small,
I knew to keep my ear close to the ground.
Even now, I find I still recall
the multitude of noises to be found
as I learned about this city from its sound.

In black-out years, when I was very small
Humanity was facing some decline,
civilization was heading for a fall;
so often we would hear the siren's whine
that meant we had to hurry underground.
I came to know this city from such sound.

I knew to keep my ear close to the ground,
took careful note of everything I learned.
The sights I saw so often would astound;
I glimpsed them at each corner that I turned.
Yet images can frequently confound
and I came to know this city from its sound.

Even now, I find I still recall
the rattling of trams along the street.
The murmurs of the night held me in thrall;

I listened for the features they'd repeat;
east and west, north and southbound;
I recognized this city by such sound.

The multitude of noises to be found;
Factories roar and church bells chime;
the throb of human traffic all around
from break of day to closing time.
My perception then was so profound
I learned to love my city from its sound.

## Caithness Sabbath Morn

So still and silent! One expects to hear
the scud of clouds as they roll by.
The sun shines bright, the air is clear
while above us, in the towering sky
there's nothing there to tease the ear;
*not a whisper, not a sigh*

Wavelets softly lap the shore
like some gentle lullaby
that stills the mighty ocean's roar.
Last night the wind began to die
and now its howl is heard no more;
*not a whisper, not a sigh.*

Once we've risen, washed and dressed,
hung all our worries out to dry,
Our Town puts on its Sunday best,
and walks to worship, pledged to try
to utter, on this day of rest,
*not a whisper, not a sigh.*

## An Old Man's Death

I dread to die an old man's death
and mean to fight until the end
to save my wits, my strength, my breath.

With dignity, I will defend
those inner feelings that sustain
my conscious self. I'll not depend

on mere good fortune to maintain
faculties that I still require;
my imagination and my brain.

My instinct, memory and desire
are qualities on which I must rely
to serve the goals to which I still aspire.

Such weapons will allow me to defy
that old man's death that I refuse to die.

## Young Isa's Blues

When Isa was young, there was no radio;
No gramophone records, certainly no
tickets for the theatre to see a travelling show.

Young Isa had the music, the gift of song.
For the others at her workplace, the usual throng
She'd read from any sheet they might bring along.

Her singing was quite popular, but enjoyed no fame.
In spite of all her talent, it was such a crying shame
that, outside of the factory, nobody knew her name.

Yet Isa was never interested in that kind of thing;
She wasn't looking for stardom – she just wanted to sing.

## Jessie

Your luminous beauty lingers still
in the bosom of my memory.
I never could and never will
forget how very much you meant to me.

Exhausted, fevered, very ill,
I languished in extremity.
You nursed me with such tender skill
restored my every faculty.

The song you sang gave me a thrill,
a subtle kind of threnody;
and, even now, my eyes can fill
should I hear that haunting melody.

As years go by, my memories chill
           – but your luminous beauty lingers still

# Black Jean

*In Memoriam Jane Sutherland Mackenzie*

It's the gentleness that I still recall;
the kindly smile that twinkled on her face;
the wondrous warmth of her embrace;
the music of her laughter most of all.

The dignity that never knew disgrace;
the humour that she never thought to hide;
the courage that refused to be denied;
the strength no hardship ever could efface.

At the start, she was my only guide;
the first to teach me right from wrong.
This memory is still where I belong.
Even now, her shade walks by my side.

Making sure my dreams stay sure and strong,
her spirit sings within me like a song.

## Godless in Gorgie

God has gone away from Gorgie now.
No longer do the church bells ring.
Life has become quite dark somehow.

The memories to which we cling
are all completely maladjusted.
We've made a mess of everything.

There's no one left who can be trusted
to share a joke or raise a cheer.
Humour's gone, enthusiasm rusted.

My boyhood greets me with a sneer,
confirming what I've long suspected;
my old friends are no longer here,
The people now seem disconnected.
Our community has clearly passed away.
Even the buildings seem dejected.

On the streets no children play
And no one comes to sweep them clean.
The massage parlour and the takeaway

Now uglify our ageing urban scene.
The cinema and chip-shop are no more
and everything is beggarly and mean.

Poor as we might have been before
We always had a furrow we could plough.
Jobless, people now have nothing left in store,

Nothing seems to matter anyhow.
As the district descends in deep despair
the Devil dances on this thoroughfare
and God has gone away from Gorgie now.

## Austerity Chant

Who will draw the water?
*Who will hew the wood?*
*Who will build our shelter?*
*Who will grow the food?*
*Who will forge the steel?*
*Who will nurse and heal?*
*Who will bear the loads?*
*Who will bake the bread?*
*Who will mend the roads?*
*Who will bury the dead?*
*Who will guard the cities?*
*Who will walk the beats?*
*Who will sing the ditties?*
Who will sweep the streets?

When all such savings have been made
to put more millions in the pot,
which of us can then be paid
when there's nothing that can be bought?

## Salt of the Earth

Last thing at night, he liked to shave.
Always keen to start at break of day.
This is the way he would behave
before they came and took his job away

He thought nothing of the time he'd save.
His main concern was always with his trade.
No-one ever told him he was just a slave
with no right to the profit his work made.

Before they came and took his job away
and stole the wage on which his home relied,
his work meant so much more than simply pay.
It was a daily duty that could never be denied.

Always keen to start at break of day,
the best he had was what he always gave.
Eager to begin without the least delay,
last thing at night, he always liked to shave.

# Uncollected Poems

These are poems that have appeared in various outlets since the publication of my *Selected Poems in 1990*. These are the fugitive pieces from which this collection takes its title.

# The Wonderful World of Ned Holt

## Street Characters of Victorian Edinburgh

## Kirsty Davidson

Kirsty Davidson must walk slow;
her back is bent, her legs unsteady.
Each step takes time, she'll only go
                     when she is ready.

Down Causewayside she makes her way
to Anderson's delightful shop.
When Kirsty has the means to pay
                     she likes a drop.

She'll sup her drink amid the hum
of company and soon regain
her spirits and, once more become
                     herself again,

A six-year-old at play upon the street;
a sweet young girl seen dancing at a ball;
an older woman quick upon her feet;
                     Kirsty is them all.

Her neighbours love her – she can be sure
at closing-time they'll rally round
to see her home to her own front-door
safe and sound.

## Sour Ale

This sad young man, inclined to sin
Imagined it was masculine
To drink strong liquor to excess
And so began in idleness
A battle he could never win.

It wasn't whisky, rum or gin
That brought about the state he's in,
But simply ale, drunk sour and thin
From barrel or from can,
That dumped his prospects in the bin,
This sad young man.

With sour ale stinking through his skin
And slobbering all down his chin,
Ignored by friends, despised by kin,
He badly needs another plan
But little knows where to begin,
This sad young man.

## Black Mary

Black Mary of the Happy Land
was sometimes hard yet always fair.
Let Leith Wynd lodgers understand
they'd find no trace of softness there.

Strong liquor she could never bear
And laudanum was likewise banned.
No bully boys could ever scare
Black Mary of the Happy Land.

Her neighbours knew her to be kind;
As kind as you'd find anywhere.
Even so, the Lady of Leith Wynd
Was sometimes hard, yet always fair.

Kindness aside, she never planned
To shelter those in deep despair
The lodgers of the Happy Land
Would find no trace of softness there.

## Apple Glory

Friend of the famous and the fair,
Apple Glory kept her stall
for many a year on Shakespere Square
where everybody knew the call
of her sweet voice, that beatific smile,
a style beloved by one and all.

## Willie Thomas

Willie Thomas seems dismayed;
he hardly knows where he must start
to recoup all that he has paid.
His goods are rotting on his cart.
There's no more profit to be made
Dear Apple Glory, so appealing
is stealing all her uncle's trade

## Coconut Tam

A bread and butter life at best
With little sugar, far less jam
Yet, in the High Street, with the rest
Of his wild kind, he bore the palm.
*Taste and try afore ye buy!*
That was the cry of Coconut Tam.

## Jamie Sprigens

Jamie Sprigens loves to dance
as others love to sing
and anytime he gets the chance
he'll put down sticks for swords and prance
out the steps of the Highland Fling.
Despite his ragged circumstance
how Jamie Sprigens loves to dance...
Oh! Almost more than anything!

## Tory Gunn

Look out for him, he's often seen
strutting smartly round the town.
He's a soldier of the Queen;
a loyal servant of the Crown

He'll promise any lad who's willing
a pint of ale to take the shilling
and be a soldier of the Queen.
a loyal servant of the Crown.

Peacock-proud, he's hard and mean
and full of tricks to nail you down.
So mind and take this warning, son;
Never take a drink from Tory Gunn!

 Look out for him, he's often seen
strutting smartly round the town.

# *Joe Co'burn*

As brave as brave could be
Young Joe Co'burn went to sea
in loyal service of his native land.
Yet Jane was always on his mind;
that sweet lass he left behind.
He wore her golden ring on his left hand.

Later on Joe was to find
Jane was not the waiting kind;
patience played no part in her life's plan.
When Joe came home from the sea
with his leg shot off at the knee
he discovered that she'd wed another man.

Here he is now, destitute,
Having lost his good right foot,
as unhappy as a sparrow that can't sing.
To make matters so much worse,
being mindful of her purse,
Jane demanded the return of her gold ring.

## Old Cherry

Old Cherry knows the road to take
For any journey you might make,
whether for worship, work or play.
Rely on him; he knows the way.

For forty years, in his old brake
he's worked this city night and day;
He knows each corner, bend and brae.
He'll do his best to get you there,
no matter how great or small the fare.
His duty's done for duty's sake.

Yet time moves on; his old bones ache;
so quickly now he seems to tire.
He can no longer ply for hire
and so, although his heart might break
Old Cherry knows the road to take

## Reverend Beily

He needs a mask to hide the grin
that hovers just above his chin,
His congregation must not see
the least degree of levity,
the humour shining deep within.

His firm belief in discipline
Must always seek to underpin
the preaching of his ministry.
His people, in extremity,
All know quite well his suit of black
signifies that true divinity
of which he has no lack.
Yet, to be equal to his task
 he needs a mask.

## Doctor Goodall

"Doctor Goodall is not keeping well"
That's what all his patients say.
How did he come to seem so frail?

Look at him; you can clearly tell.
Doctor Goodall is not keeping well.
His voice is weak and his skin is grey.

He'll come at once, without fail
when needed, and he won't delay.
That's what all his patients say.

He works too hard; it's all pell-mell.
'Patients to see.' – that old cliché
Doctor Goodall is not keeping well.

He badly needs a holiday.
That's what all his patients say.

## Mrs. Hare

No-one believed she never knew
the nature of her husband's game.
Her innocence did not ring true.
It was clear that she bore some blame.

Burke and Hare caused so much pain;
this nightmare she was living through,
They killed and killed and killed again,
No-one believed she never knew.

Poverty, her constant guest
made every day seem much the same.
Small wonder that she never guessed
the nature of her husband's game.

The money she received from Hare
she took as only her just due.
How could she then be unaware?
Her innocence did not ring true.

She must have guessed his guilt sometimes.
She shared his bed and shared his name;
She shared the profit of his crimes
so it was clear that she bore some blame.

# To poets

# Romantic Town

*A Ballade for Poethon '91*

When last, I wonder, did Auld Reekie ring
through every hour and minute of the day
with such a rolling round of rhyme, to sing
down every thoroughfare, up every brae?

We pass the poems around in swift relay
of striking verb, reverberating noun.
We vivify the very air with spoken poetry.

As Edinburgh again assumes the golden crown
of Festival, our epic roundelay,
our Poethon of pleasure, passion and renown
strips this precipitous city of its hodden gray
and resurrects our own romantic town.

## Clear Fire

*To Hugh MacDiarmid on his eightieth birthday*

Licht. There has aye to be licht.
Simple answers, we're aften tellt,
are guid eneuch for the honest speiring o simple men
– and the truth, according to Oscar, is
"never pure and rarely simple"
Deid wrang exactly! The plain fact is
that the truth (while never simple)
can whiles be pure.

Licht is truth at its purest.

Yet new dawns aye kyth cannily
for just as any man roused
frae a hard nicht on the bottle finds
water owre wersh and sound owre strang
just sae the new licht blinds – and syne becomes
a murky glare for sichtless men tae boggle at.

Thus, frae the carriers o licht no the easiest

o prices *are* demanded. There have to be coals
to kindle and hands to lay them on, hands
that have baith the virr tae hold the burning wecht
an the smeddum to tak nae tent
o aa the scarts that sic a job will shairly bring.

Licht. There has aye tae be licht
but at the hinner end
there has aye tae be fire tae create it.

Leave it at this. That I,
coming to life at the hicht o your trauchle
ettle to dae mair nor ferlie at the burning need
this cauld an damp an dark world has for the fire
you wrocht an carry yet intil the ninth decade;
and raxing through my sichtless age, maun tyauve anaa
tae kep ae saving glimmer o thon michty lowe
that never will be smorrit and within ye bides
auchty-year auld and eternally ablaze.

# Blues for a Gay Makar

*An elegy for Edwin Morgan (1920 – 2010)*

Puir auld dear!
He'd looking sairly vexed
Sitting in his rocking chair
Puzzled and perplexed.
They want him to speak:
But there's nathing he wants to say.
All over the city they're giving his poems away

His poetic career
could never compensate
for the fasherie and fear
of his homosexual state.
They leave him his lane
For a price he's unwilling to pay.
All over the city they're giving his poems away

*Giving his poems away!*
*Sending his dreams on a holiday!*
*Love lives in a kirk*
*where he's never learned how to pray.*
*All over the city they're giving his poems away*

It's very clear
He's lang been celibate
Missing the guid cheer
Of a lover or a mate.

He'd sooner be straight
But how can he help being gay?
All over the city they're giving his poems away

Some like to sneer
And cry him reprobate,
Fairy, poof and queer. ..
This leaves him desolate
Sic bigots aye deny
A truth they can never gainsay
*In every part of the city they're learning his poems today.*

# Thinking of Norman MacCaig (1910 -1995)

*Sonnets in Celebration of his Centenary, November 2010,*

## Solsgirth 1972

Returning from Solsgirth on the bus that night,
 you suddenly turned obnoxious as we shared
 the last of the whisky. Your eyes grew bright

And your face flushed as you wildly glared
at me in anger, spouting all kinds of abuse
in my direction. For a moment, I was scared

By this indication that some screw had broken loose
Of course, it was no more than just a flash that flared
for a moment – and nothing I could say would be of use

in damping down the flames, even if I had cared
enough to try to guide you through it.
And why should I? Already I had spared

Your blushes. Gutted by grief, you nearly blew it.
Your dignity was saved that night – and you knew it.

## Dundee 1982

On the morning we lost Geerie, our pawkie wee pal,
we set off from Haymarket en route to Dundee
To fulfil our engagement at the Bonar Hall.

There was nobody else, just you and me
And the reading itself was somewhat routine.
We started at two, finished up at half- three

Then went off for a stroll on the Magdalen Green
where we sat on a bench and had a long talk
regarding our chums on the poetry scene.

The best of the brethren we were bound to miss –
our conversation remembered them then.
There was Geerie and Sydney, but most of all Chris ...

"Oh, come on, boy!" you winced, as if in pain,
"Let's leave this. I have to go and be MacCaig again."

## Perth, 1992

Trout at the Torino, followed by the sweet
Taste of Glenmorangie, before
Taking a taxi to Craigie, there to meet

Your patient public, just under a score
Of teenage schoolgirls, dressed to kill,
Purring with delight as you took the floor.

What a night! I remember still
the magic of that occasion,
The collective sigh, the vibrant thrill

Of joy and jubilation, the raw elation
in your voice at the evening's end.
"That was a great celebration.

I might have known I could depend
on you, boy. Thanks a lot, my friend."

## Gilmour Place, 2010

The other day I saw your ghost
sauntering along Gilmour Place
He did not speak, but simply tossed

his head in passing. That handsome face
seemed quite composed, with cigarette
in hand as he came sidling out of space.

My dear old dominie from former days
whose scathing wit I never can forget
has gone forever and of course there was no trace

of his ego or his temperament.
Only such qualities as Death cannot erase.
his style and substance, were still evident

as he proceeded at that pleasant pace,
charming us all with a most uncommon grace.

And more...

## Thon Hoose

I'll no gang back to thon hoose,
thon sad auld, bad auld
hame for the hard and hairtless
that brocht birth til us baith:
my life and your daith
- t'ane thrawn, t'ither airtless –
found nae favour siccan a place.

In our aucht belangs another hoose
where nane can say us nay.
With rooms aneuch to gie us scouth,
ablow its cosy, hairtsome roof
we'll find ourselves, provide the proof
that we maun be as guid as they
that suck our substance, steal our use.

Tak tent of this and let the lave
gang where it wills –
the human spirit's no a slave
that makes nae mair nor kirks and mills.
Plaster, slates and stane
want for muckle in love and grace.
I canna gang back to thon hoose
- thon hoose was never our ain.

## 12 Vansittart Street.

It was siccar then
And it's siccar nou;
an ile-lamp alowe in my minding,

The room, the fowk, the furniture,
the strang stair rising
to the Land o the Leal in the garret.

*The parritch-stick is turning yet,*
*The fire is roaring rarely;*
*Somebody's singing "Danny Boy";*
*Anither voice is greeting sairly.*

For there's aye the slated shed,
Satan-black wi mystery;
A soughing o coal that fyles my bluid.
There's aye the road I winna gang,
Aye the gate I canna pass,
Aye the word I'll never speak.

The ile burns sair in my minding and winna be smorit
     ever.

*It's as siccar nou as it was siccar then,*

## Whispers.

For all I canna
Ken ye, ye're aye near,
touching me in whispers.

Owre uncharted waters,
dark as December,
I'll follow your lead.

Fever whiles burns;
I thole its discomfort
through your remedy.

The days o the bully
Syndit my fears
In your bonniest hankie.

We learn our lessons;
When the schule skailt
I hurried hame wi your prizes.

*Your man, my woman;*
*My sons, your dochters;*
*Your daith, my living.*

Yestreen, I heard ye
Whisper in my ear
Seven verses o this poem.

## Sandra Dancing.

Gin I could see our Sandra dancing
I'd shed the tears I canna find
and all the years I meet advancing
I'd no be sweirt to leave behind.

I'd shed the tears I canna find,
smash thon hairt that winna break.
I'd no be sweirt to leave behind
my fantasies, for Sandra's sake.

Smash thon hairt that winna break!
Time alane wad mend the smairt.
My fantasies, for Sandra's sake
wad honour my resurgent hairt.

Time alane wad mend the smairt.
My dreams wad aye be born again,
wad honour my resurgent hairt,
wad ease my sorrow, heal my pain.

My dreams wad aye be born again
and all the years I meet advancing
wad ease my sorrow, heal my pain
- gin I could see our Sandra dancing.

## My Faither's Son

Whiles I feel like my faither;
a canny man wha aye took tent
to haud his hairt and heid thegither
with toil and trust and sentiment.

He hated greed, loved tradition
and, all his days, he never kent
ae stound of envy or ambition.
Looking out for number one
was aye, for him, a fause position.

My deeds betray his benison
and, in my blood, my needs foregather
to feed a thocht I maunna shun.

*Whiles, I feel like my faither.*
*For ordnar, I maun mind I'm his son.*

## Free and Easy

Deep in my dreams of history
My Grandad sings his sangs to me
In Bryce's Bar on Princes Street
Where bonnie lads and lassies meet

Sae crously they foregather there.
With Norman Thomson in the Chair,
Ye'll rarely find an empty seat
In Bryce's Bar on Princes Street.

Syne, at nine, the gavel chaps
And "Best of Order!" Norman snaps.
As lassies their braw laddies meet,
My Grandad rises to his feet

With Johnny Inglis in the middle
And Willie Sangster on the fiddle,
The band provides an unco treat
When bonnie lads and lassies meet.

*It's free and easy there, ye see;*
*a place fair filled with gaiety*
*where chambermaids and gallus caddies,*
*clerkesses and sailor-laddies,*
*Jenners' quines and Piershill squaddies,*
*all toshed up in the latest thing,*

*have come to hear my Grandad sing*
*in sic a blythesome-like retreat*
*where lassies and their lads can meet.*

Sic merriment was sair brocht doun
One Sarajevo afternoon
Lassies nou nae laddies meet
In Bryces Bar on Princes Street.

Yet in a voice that's warm and sweet,
virrsome aneuch to gar ye greet
my Grandad sings his sangs to me
as free and easy as can be!

# In Pulteney Again

Afore ye kent what logic was
or heard what understanding spoke,
ye heard the voices of your hairt
Amang the clashing of your folk

Afore the rising and the fall,
the stab of truth, the drug of lies,
ye sang the music of your soul
upon sic streets, aneath sic skies

Afore the pleasure and the pain,
Afore life swung on what was said,
ye caught the images of art
in every tone sic voices bred

After the struggle and the fight,
after the story and the song,
ye'll touch again your ain true voice
- and ken for sure where we belong

## John Badbea

A follower of Gair and Grant,
Auld John Badbea was a sage
whase life was rarely free of want.

Bauchie in bairnheid, frail in auld age,
his witness borne in constant pain,
his days were sair at every stage.

Gales micht roar and seas micht rage,
as hardship hammered at his door.
Its sound and fury proved in vain.

Through tempest, storm and hurricane
the thocht of glory he'd disdain.
Auld John kent fine he'd stand the strain.

Life's squalls micht shake his very core
His faith aye kept him to the fore.

# Prince Marmaduke

*A Tale of a Pussycat*

Marmaduke rules. He kens O.K.
There's no' a game he canna play.
In this, his ain wee pussy beat,
*He's* cock o' the green, king o' the street.

A kitten cat, sae braw and sleek,
He'd tell ye this, gin he could speak.
There was a time (and no lang since)
When Marmie was a *real* prince!

Sitting in state in his pavilion,
He ruled his subjects by the million.
And law and kirk and schule and army
Aa peyed their due respect til Marmie!

Ae day, this wicked witch arrived
And, when she saw the kingdom thrived,
It scunnered her. She took her book
And cast a spell on Marmaduke!

'A pussy-cat ye'll be!' she skirled.
'And need tae trauchle through this world.
Ye'll mooch aboot frae street tae street
And hunt the causeys for your meat!'

So there ye are. Is it no' strange?
There's things e'en magic canna change.
The form is different, no' the nature.
Marm's yet a handsome, royal creature.

Ablow my windae, ilka day
I watch him rin and sport and play.
He's no' as great as he was aince
-but Marmaduke is still a prince!

Marmaduke rules! He kens O.K.
there's no' a game he canna play.
In this, his ain wee pussy beat,
he's cock o' the green, king o' the street!

## Old Man Dreaming

When I was young, I had this dream
featuring my future's theme;
where I'd go and what I'd see,
when I'd grow and who I'd be,
what part I'd play in life's grand scheme.

As years passed by, I struggled through
and did the best that I could do.
Sometimes I failed
but luck prevailed
and so, at last, my dream came true.

*I made the rhymes*
*Endured the mimes,*
*Employed the hooks*
*and wrote the books*
*that tell the story of my times.*

Another fancy's now begun,
albeit quite a different one.
My future's past,
I'm free at last
to dream of all I might have done.

## Jenny Clow

The lass that kissed the poet's brow
Lies cold and lifeless in the grave.
There are no songs for Jenny Clow,

Afore she perished with the lave
She earned her bread out on the street.
She was a vauntie lass and brave

In business, she was aye discreet.
Never so blate, she whiles seemed shy.
Her voice was warm, her smile was sweet

A shame that such a lass should die
when Johnnie Richmond broke his vow.
No poet, he – and that is why
There are no songs for Jenny Clow,

## Sonnet for Elizabeth

Amang the auld, Elizabeth bears
the hasteless hours with an ill grace,
grudging the thocht that she maun spend

her hindmaist days in this pitied place
where nocht but bodies bide: an end
she never socht has taen her unawares.

Yet, in her een, there kythes a trace
of licht, undaunted, that declares
Elizabeth alive. She'll no pretend

contentment nor let bad taste offend
a sense of dignity her ninety-seven years
maintain. Her sairly trauchled race

is geynear run, yet still she bravely dares
defy her dotage with a fair, forbidding face.

## Royal Wave

*A somonka for Donald Smith*

Her Majesty, our noble Queen,
riding in her limousine
doun the Canongait, is seen
by a gang of gallus lassies
wha cheer as, with a wave,
she passes.

As we baith stare
it wad be utterly fair
to say there's magic in the air.
Even so, our reverence grows slack
we stand our ground
and wave right back!

## Keelie Kyrielle

Our Scotland's wanting still the choice
of Government. Maun we rejoice
in thralldom as we stir the shit?
*Thank God! I feel some keelie in me yet!*

Kirk elders in another guise
Now rule the roost. It's no surprise
Their deeds are sic as make ye spit.
*Thank God! l feel some keelie in me yet!*

The chattering class on the air
Aye tell the tale. It's unco clear
They ken the words but want the wit
*Thank God! I feel some keelie in me yet!*

Our puppet poets tak tent to muse
In fields true makars aye refuse.
Their fearful rhymes just canna fit
*Thank God! l feel some keelie in me yet!*

The common folk gar me despair.
They ken what's richt, yet winna dare
Take owre the reins, rule over it.
*Thank God! I feel some keelie in me yet!*

Myself, I ken, am just the same
As all the rest. I share the blame.
I'm feart and lazy, apathetic yet
*Thank God! I feel some keelie in me yet!*

## April 1992

Scunnered by my cringing kind;
I think of Lermontov and find
his thocht reflected in my ain
sair generation; thowless, blind;
trauchled at hairt, troubled in mind.

Our thwarted faithers' saikless gain
was our deid loss. They took the strain,
leaving us little but ease.
Spared of hardship, puirtith, pain;
we think to thrive on breid alane

and squander living as we'd please;
our passions blaze, our spirits freeze
in *dolce far niente*. We canna tell
guid frae evil – and, on our knees,
we tine our manhood by degrees.

Sae feared of failure, we dispel
each dream of liberty and sell
our birthricht cheaply, run
away frae victory; compel
our consciences to snore in hell!

Our lives maun end as they begun
with muckle lost and nathing won;
history aince mair repeated;
the past betrayed, the future cheated,
the promise of our age undone
disgraced, dishonoured and defeated.

## The Alliterative Street Pedlar

An aged, artful apron is my arm,
Bedecked with baubles bountiful and bold,
Caressed with creative characters of charm,
Delightful dollies, dashing, deft, and droll.
Everlasting, elves escape my eyes,
(For fairies flutter faraway in fear)
Ghastly giants grunt in gaping guise,
Hurry homeward, hardly halt to hear.
Illiterate intruders inch inside,
Jolt my jaws and jeopardize my jokes.
Kinky knuckled kneesies and their kind
Lacerate my lanterns with their locks.
My metier is marvellous and made,
Never nudging nobility or nuns;
Overtly offering overcoats ornate,
Plying plastic parasols with puns.
Quaint and querulous queanagies from Quant
Rosily roll around me in the rain
Sexy summer slip-ons, so slyly sibilant,
Tarted up for titillation and disdain.
Understanding universal urks,
Veering off in volumes vast and vexed,
Wondering where to weasel out the works,
Expecting extra xenons from the Ex.
Yellow, yawning youth my only yen,
Zippy in a zestful zigzag Zend.

## Scottie's Song

I never wear a kilt or plaid or tammy
and Harris tweed just leaves me feeling blue.
I'm not much for heather
and I can't stand the weather!
Still and all
I'm Scottish through and through.

I've never been much good at country dancing.
Of Scottish songs I only know a few.
Poetry ignores me.
Robbie Burns just bores me.
Still and all
I'm Scottish through and through.

At Halloween and Hogmanay
and even on St. Andrew's Day
I join in the celebration.
And when the band begins to play
I always stand for "Scots Wha Hae"

*I'll shout it loud – I'm so very proud*
*To be part of this wonderful nation,*

Football is a game I've never favoured.
My ignorance of golf just isn't true.
and when they toss the caber

I hide behind a neighbour
Still and all
I'm Scottish through and through.

I've never been to Oronsay
or Stornoway or Colonsay.
I've never been to Thurso or to Troon
To Galloway or Alloway
and, by the way, just let me say
I'd never get a part in *Brigadoon*!

Don't tell me that it really doesn't matter
where I was born or even where I grew!
I could live without it
but can't do much about it.
No matter what
I'm Scottish, through and through!
There you go –
          I'm Scottish, just like you!

## Words in Comfort

*For any poet.*

After all this talk has perished
the wounds are forgotten and the legends blown
away re-moulded and re-struck anew.
When the earth has made grass
of the battlements of your conceits
When your arguments have been confounded
by other arguments, your visions refurbished
and re-represented as newer visions.
When your quarrels have become dust
When your affections are laid side by side
as nothing with your insecurities
when they take down your tombstone
to repair the cemetery wall
Where will you be?
And what will all this chatter mean then?

Or does it matter?
Are any of these questions relevant?
No one today remembers – few even know –
that Yessenin was clownish or Verlaine sly
in their respective hypocrisies. No one
cares that Francois Villon murdered
Dylan Thomas drank like thunder
Robert Burns beat
Jean Armour without mercy and a curious
kind of joy.

And so it will be with your own weaknesses.
Time will take all and no one will blame you.
All that may be remembered is that once
in the darkness of your wildest dream
you perhaps muttered
a few words that were somehow right
and somehow in their straight and proper order.

# Translations

These poems mostly have there origins in the dissatisfaction I have felt with previous translations which tend to concentrate on literal meaning at the expense of poetic effect. Wherever possible, I have gone back to the original language in an attempt to do the poetry justice.

# Poems from the Native
# American Nations

Poems from the Native American Nations. These all appear in *An Anthology of World Poetry* (ed. Mark Van Doren, Cassel & Co.,1929.) My versions are adaptations of the translations appearing there, which are obviously literal.

# Serenade

(from *Neither Spirit nor Bird* by Mary Austin in Shoshone)

Didn't you hear me sing last night?
as you made your way in the fading light
with your pail down to the river?
That wasn't the wind, that wasn't a bird.
That was the sound of my voice you heard,
the serenade of your lover.

As you came stepping through the grass
so daintily, I saw you pass,
the riverbank your beauty gracing.
If, near at hand, you heard a stirring
like some big cat strongly purring,
you should not fear.

The rhythmic sound you heard repeating
was no more than my heart beating,
to find you near.

Surely then, you heard me whistle
as your movement's fragrant rustle
shook my heart, set my blood racing?

## Callous Lover

(from *Come not Near my Songs* by Mary Austin in Shoshone)

Take good care, my callous lover,
when you drive me to despair.
My verse, as you may soon discover,
is like to catch you unawares.

Like a flash of forest fire,
a quickening desire,
an unexpected pain,
a sudden shower of rain,
my verses, when you don't detect them
will leap out when you least expect them

The wounds inflicted on my heart
just sweeten with their bruising.
They stimulate the poet's art
And fortify my musing.
Relentlessly my verses run
to flush you from your cover.
     They'll seek you out and hunt you down
     - so best beware, my callous lover.

# A Prayer to the Sun

(from *Song for Fine Weather* by Constance Lindsay Skinner in Haida)

Shine on, sweet Sun, fill up our day
and keep those thick black clouds away,
satisfying every wish
of those who go to hunt and fish.
Let all our people live in peace,
all enmity between us cease
and harmony forever reign.
Again, again and then again
ease our burdens, please our play
until every difficulty is gone
Shine on, sweet Sun, shine on, shine on.

## The Mountain Path

(from *Song to the Mountain* by Alice C. Fisher in Pawnee)

The mountain road is the path we take.
It lies before us, steep and clear.
This is the journey we must make.

It means a climb without a break
We make our way up there from here.
The mountain road is the path we take.

Our hearts grow weary, muscles ache;
The peak above looms proud and clear.
This is the journey we must make

The mountain road is the path we take;
Step follows step, so slow, we fear
Yet See! The summit's growing near!
We'll rest and sing our songs up here.
This is the journey all must make.

# Lament of a Father

(from *Lament of a Man for his Son* by Mary Austin in Paiute)

Oh, my son, my son, my beloved son!
What will life hold for me, now you are gone?

I will carry my sorrow to the height
of the mountain and there I will light
a fire to warm your spirit.

*Oh, my son, my son, my beloved son!*
What will life hold for me, now you are gone?

Robed as a chief, with his weapons to hand
he walks today in the spirit land
where all may know his merit.

*Oh, my son, my son, my beloved son!*
 What will life hold for me, now you are gone?

The corn may come to the ear again
but, like an empty stalk that's left in the rain
my grief is all I inherit.

*Oh, my son, my son, my beloved son!*
What will life hold for me, now you are gone?

## Tanka

(from *Lovesong* by Mary Austin in Papago)

As the dawn comes creeping
my lover wakes
me up from my sleeping
as the blue morning breaks.
On Papago Mountain, deer-calves at play
look into my eyes in much the same way.

## Cinquain

(from *The Coyote and the Locust* by Frank Cushing in Zuni)

All day long
Playing his flute
The locust clings to the pines
Beneath a brilliant sun that shines
All day long.

## Love Englyn

(from *Lovesong* by Constance Lindsay Skinner in Haida)

Like the fragrant flowers that grow
on the sunlit mountainside,
her surface beauty shines, a glow
of warmth that cannot be denied.
Yet, like the mountain's bank of snow
she's frozen deep inside.

# The Cottonwood's Song

(from *A Lover's Lament* by H.J. Spinden in Tewa)

Remember, love, when we were young,
We'd meet down by the flowing stream
and listen to the cottonwood's song.

Even now, I feel a sudden gleam
of tears come to my eyes
as I recall our lost love's dream.

On summer days beneath blue skies
on flower-decked meadows as we strolled
Heartbreak arrived in Love's disguise.

As green fields ripened  into gold
and leaf-birds sang in the morning sun
I shivered as your love grew cold.

It's not the same, love. Since you've gone
I walk those crimson fields alone.

## *Bear Song*

(from *The Bear's Song* by Constance Lindsay Skinner in Haida)

This woman I've taken to wife
is worthy of every praise.
I'll defend her with my life,
with my axe, my bow and my knife.
She'll cause neither trouble or strife.
Despite what her family say
this woman I've taken to wife
I'll cherish the rest of my days.

## *Beautiful Land*

(from *The Voice that Beautifies the Land* by Washington Matthews
in Navaho)

How beautifully the land lies under
the flash of lightning, crash of thunder.
Dark clouds can only serve to grace
the pleasures of this special place
that fills our hearts with so much wonder.

As beautiful, the land below.
In meadows where the sweet flowers grow,
larks rise at dawn in sheer delight
and crickets chirrup at twilight.
A paradise is here on show;
a beautiful country we all know

## *Faraway, the Rain*

(from *Song of the Rain Chant* by Natalie Curtis in Navaho)

Faraway the rain comes over
like some sad, repentant lover.
From the mountain we can see
its showers approaching gradually

Flash of lightning is the other
sign our watching eyes discover,
warning that the rain is nigh
as it zig-sags in the sky.

The swallows flee before the weather,
screaming as they flock together.
and, as far as eyes can see
the rain comes on relentlessly

It puts the pollen in a lather;
there's little left for bees to gather
A healing rain comes rushing down
to feed the fields where crops are grown

Faraway, the rain is seen
This dusty land will soon turn green.
Enriching harvests in the sun
we'll know when rain has come and gone.

# Song in Springtime

(from *Korosta Katzina Song* by Natalie Curtis in Navaho)

Among the springtime corn
yellow butterflies are playing,
chasing in a joyful swarm
great clouds of pollen spraying.
And nearby, where the sweet beans grow
their blue brothers do the same;
racing one and other to and fro
in a bright, unbroken stream.

Up above, wild bees are humming
and the darkness of the skies
means a downpour will be coming
and we all must realize
raindrops will be drumming
down before the close of day
when corn and beans and butterflies
will all be washed away.

# Blackbird's Hunting Song

(from *Huntingsong by* Natalie Curtis in Navaho)


I'm the blackbird, hear my song!
I sing to the deer all day.
*Dainty deer, will you come along?*
*Come along and follow me!*


I watch them grazing on the mountainside,
*I sing to the deer all day*
and it fills my heart with so much pride
*Come along and follow me!*


Herding together, a wonderful sight
*I sing to the deer all day.*
with their dappled coats and their eyes so bright
*Come along and follow me!*


They won't take fright but stop and stare
*Come along and follow me!*
Standing high on the Mountain stair!
*I sing to the dainty deer all day!*


*Come along, come along and follow me!*
*Come along, come along and follow me!*
*Help me to feed my family.*

# Other Translations

## Sally Grant

From the Gaelic of Rob Donn

Lang afore I first saw ye,
I'd heard tell of your fame.
*She's bonnie, blythesome and young.*
Like a goddess, they cried ye;
folk knelt at your name.
*Ye're bonnie, blythesome and young.*
Weill, I kent it was sooth,
nothing less nor the truth
when the music started to play.
Every word I'd been tellt
was weill-proven, I felt
by the sicht of ye dancing so gay
*And bonnie, blythesome and young.*


Oh, the Colonel maun never
make Sally his wife.
*She's bonnie, blythesome and young.*
Gin he did, all the others
would loathe him for life!
*So bonnie, blythesome and young.*
A female so fine,
sic a damsel divine....
Losh, what a shame it would be
gin a woman whose worth

grants sic grace to the earth
didna bide single and free
*And bonnie, blythesome and young.*

Says George, the auld stager,
It's lang been weill-kent
*She's bonnie, blythesome and young.*
At marriage, the Major
has served a lang stint
*She's bonnie blythesome and young.*
Yet when the drink's in
and he sits himself doun
every pint at the table is savoured
with sic a braw boast.
All the ladies he'll toast
forby Sally, fairly feel favoured
*And bonnie, blythesome and young.*

# Merkin Cairn

From the Gaelic of Rob Donn, *A dialogue between sisters.*

## Mary

Why should a well-bred girl like me
risk her health, going up the hill
to Merkin Cairn especially?
The very thought makes me feel ill.
That so-called fair has no proper
stalls that might offer what I require;
A few spoons and occasional copper
litter the floor of the byre.

## Isobel

The British monarch owns no space
that suits me nearly so well
as the Cairn, that magical place
where young girls may spend a spell
in tranquillity and seclusion,
sampling any sound that they desire;
pasture, trees, flowers in profusion
with all the colours they require,
as the birdsong echoes merrily,
like the strings of the sweetest lyre

## Mary

It is hardly the place for the Sabbath Day;
visiting a cairn or a cave
to witness no more than a badger at play.
All year, you'll find nothing as brave!
Oh, mist of the mountain, the gloom of the glen
make for noises I never could stand.
The rage of the flood's like to drive me insane
as the grass that grows thick on the land!

## Isobel

Och, what's matter with the high
slopes? Can ye no understand
that the pasture is needful for the kye
when the calving is near at hand?
It's no bother at all for us to sit still,
facing the falls as they flow
and pour all their goodness downhill
helping the sweet grass to grow.

## Mary

Oh, in summer you may safely praise
The beauties of this rural scene;
that warmth you feel on sunlit days
will start to cool by Halloween.
As Winter chills us to the bone,
The trees long turned to brown from green,
We'll view the Strath in monotone.
Snow hides the slopes beneath its screen

## Isobel

Aye, but the land will aye abide.
The summer will keep.
until the coming of Beltane tide
when birch and hazel no longer sleep
and send their shoots to let us know
how beautiful a harvest we'll reap.
As the snowdrift melts into a stream,
Sweet, clean new life will quickly grow
And there will be calves and butter and cream.

## Mary

Your cheese-making, it appears to me
Is far from proficient.
These hills and straths would surely be
Made much more efficient
If they were harrowed and sown
As in Caithness they have done.
Personally, I'd rather be there;
The people are wise and kind and fair.
Nothing at all like this miserable place
Where low life is thriving all over
Blinding peat smoke in my face
And only turf walls for cover.

# After the Hearing

From the Gaelic of Rob Donn

Oh, see thon Court in Tongue the day?
We'll mind its verdict for a while~
Both Judge and Fiscal had their say,
missed Justice by at least a mile~
Forbes, that sleekit tod, sat there;
Big Hughie and some Southron cheil.
Three rarer rogues there never were,
to dare to doubt an honest chiel!

I'm on my way to George Macleod
- him and me aye work well together~
For rhyming sweet or ranting loud,
he's closer to me than a brother.
A man that's fit enough to give
they twisters answer for their work,
I've no doubt; now, he waits for me
in thon wee howff ahint the kirk.

## *Aw, you!*

From the Russian of Vladimir Mayakovsky

Aw you...
Ye werenae feart!
Ye came determined
set
undaunted
(a female Abednego!)
intil the flames
the fiery furnace
o my coorse
and angry life.

Ye limmer!
Ye looked straucht
intil the ee
o my hurricane
saw
what nane ither
had seen afore
- the hert
ahint the flaming lowe
the fear
ablow the bleezing roar.

The ither quines
(Ladies o the toun!
speiring spinsters aa!)
thocht ye a ferlie
cried ye "whore"
"Love sic a loon?
Thon keelie tyke?
She maun be mad!
Afore
she kens
he'll ding her doun!"

But you?
What were ye like?
Ye didnae gie a jot
- just took haud o my hert
and gart it stot!

## Suicide Note

From the Russian of Vladimir Mayakovsky

Twelve thirty. No doubt you are in bed.
Like night, the Milky Way, the Oka's streams...
I'm in no rush
- No more telegrams! –
I'll not disturb your dreams.

Sleep tight. You will not hear a sound
From me. The affair is truly snuffed.
My craft at last has run aground.
We're even now. All sails luffed.

It doesn't matter what you said

But only look how far, how out of reach
this silence is that captivates the earth.
At such an hour, let's dedicate all speech
to mankind, history, everything of worth.

# The Ways of Wonder

After the Gaelic poem *Sligh Nan Seann Seun* of Donald Sinclair

Silence screams so shrill tonight in Paradise.
A desperate darkness streaks across Valhalla.
Passion flashes eagerly in every voice
as the ways of wonder wind westerly forever.

Bold-breasted mountains mind on auld lang syne
and a fair-faced tide turns time as in a dream,
recalling every second with a liberated whine.
Those distant days, how brave and bright they seem!

*Best of times, with customs clean and clear!*
*Happy hours of laughter, love and harmony!*
*Why is your glory now so traceless here?*
*Gracious world, gleaming with magic melody'.*

Missing the mystery that died with your departure,
No wonder hope and humour lie behind us.
A long lament sounds in the symphony of nature
and delving in the darkness all but blinds us.

The day that came to take away our kind
unheeding swallowed every scrap of certainty.
No wonder the western skies so brightly shine,
their distant dwellings staunch in their serenity.

No wonder this fertile land lies fallow.
No wonder the hills are haunted with hunger.
No wonder our songs are soaked with sorrow.
No wonder our words are wasted with anger!

*No wonder the kirkyard by the shore is still.*
*No wonder every grave with grief is filled.*

No wonder, no magic, all gone in the dust.
No word can recall it. The old ways are lost.

# Farewell to Tartan

(From the Traditional Gaelic)

Say farewell to tartan now,
dearest wishes that allow
our plaids to flourish high and low,
shining bright with tartan.

Our curses be upon the head
of King William and his seed
for making trews to serve instead
of our beloved tartan.

Below the head, those trews so gray
no pillows make at end of day.
Across the Clyde, the Lowland way
has no place for tartan.

When I was serving in the line
a kilt I had, with sporran fine;
a braw blue bonnet then was mine,
all ribboned round with tartan.

In trews, I'll never look so smart.
They'll make me play a foolish part.
How can I win a lassie's heart
if I'm not dressed in tartan?

# Notes on the Poems

## New Poems

### Godless in Gorgie

Gorgie, where the author grew up, is a working-class area of Edinburgh. It was once home to no fewer than eight places of worship. There is now only one remaining and that is poorly attended.

## Uncollected Poems

### The Wonderful World of Ned Holt

This is a selection of the poems that appeared in the exhibition of Ned Holt's paintings that took place in the Museum of Edinburgh, Huntley House, from May to June 2014.The entire exhibition can be viewed at the following website. <www.capitalcollections.org.uk>

## Apple Glory, Willie Thomas & Coconut Tam

Sarah Sibbald, better known as 'Apple Glory', ran a popular fruit stall on Shakespere Square in the days before the Theatre Royal was demolished to make way for the General Post Office. Willie Thomas was Sarah's uncle – and competitor. Thomas Paterson 'Coconut Tam' was the most celebrated Edinburgh street vendor of them all.

## Clear Fire

On the occasion of his eightieth birtday in 1972, the poet Hugh MacDiarmid was presented with a bound copy of manuscript poems from nearly every poet in Scotland. This was one of them.

## Blues for a Gay Makar

In 2007, the City of Glasgow celebrated the eighty-seventh birthday of Edwin Morgan by publishing a new selection of his poems and arranging to distribute the book gratis to Glasgow citizens. When he was interviewed on television, he seemed quite bemused by this signal honour.

## Free an Easy

This the name of an early form of Variety Theatre, usually held in the back room of a pub – known as the 'music hall'- where the author's grandfather performed regularly. The name comes from the fact that the audience were not expected to wear formal dress, as was the case in other places of entertainment at the time.

## John Badbea

Gair and Grant were leaders of "The Men", a Nineteenth Century Evangelical group in the Highlands.

## Jennie Clow

Jenny Clow was an Edinburgh prostitute who had some dealings with Robert Burns. It seems, however, that her illegitimate child was fathered, not by Burns but by his friend John Richmond.

# Translations

## Poems from the Native American Nations

These are not, strictly speaking, translations but rather metrical versions of literal translations published in the nineteen-twenties by American scholars, Mary Austin, Natalie Curtis , Washington Matthews and others.

## Sally Grant

This is the original version of this poem, predating the version that appeared in "Homage to Rob Donn."

## Merkin Cairn

This is a spot near Durness in Sutherland, where a market once took place. It was also a well-known haunt of young people of the district.

## After the Hearing

In the aftermath of the Jacobite Rebellion of 1745, the Gaelic poet Rob Donn was put on trial for composing treasonable verses. There is a tradition that he escaped a guilty verdict by improvising a verse that proved his loyalty.

# Suicide Note

This translation has been made from one of several drafts of the same poem, found among Mayakovsky's papers at the time of his suicide in 1930 and believed to have been addressed to his mistress, Lily Brik. As with "Aw You," my versions are adaptations only – I have no knowledge of Russian. The version I used is to be found in *The Bedbug and Selected Poetry*, edited by Patricia Blake (Weidenfeld and Nicholson, 1960), in which the Russian originals appear alongside translations by George Reavey and Max Hayward.

# Poems from Gaelic

The Gaelic originals for Rob Donn are to be found in *Songs and Poems in the Gaelic Language*, ed. H. Morrison, Edinburgh 1899. *The Ways of Wonder* is my translation of Donald Sinclair's *Sligh Nan Seann Seun* - to be found in *Modern Scottish Poetry*, ed Maurice Lindsay (Carcanet Press Ltd. 1976). I have worked from the original Gaelic in all cases.

# About the Poet

## Donald Campbell

Born in Caithness in 1940, Donald Campbell grew up in Edinburgh where he still lives. A full-time writer since 1974, he is active as playwright, theatre historian, stage director, script writer and poet. He is an Honorary Fellow of the Association of Scottish Literary Studies and a Life Member of the Writers' Guild of Great Britain.

Among more than a score of stage-plays, the most successful have been *The Jesuit* (1976), *The Widows of Clyth* (1979), *Blackfriars Wynd* (1980), *Till All the Seas Run Dry* (1981), *Howard's Revenge* (1985), *Victorian Values* (1986), *The Fisher Boy and the Honest Lass* (1990), *The Ould Fella* (1993) *Nancy Sleekit* (1994) and *Glorious Hearts* (1999).

Campbell made his directorial debut with a production of John McGrath's *Plugged into History* during the Edinburgh Festival of 1986. Since then, his productions have included a revival of his own

*Blackfriars Wynd*, two adaptations of Scott novels, *The Heart of Midlothian* (Edinburgh Old Town Festival, 1988) and *St. Ronan's Well* (Border Festival, 1989) a touring revival of Tom Wright's *There Was a Man* (Capstride Theatre, 1994) and the first English language version of Malin Lagerlof's *The Lighthouse Prisoner* (Northlands Festival, 1996).

As a poet, Campbell has published a substantial body of work, six full collections being represented in his *Selected Poems: 1970-1990* (Galliard, 1990). Other work includes six television plays, some fifty radio programmes, three short films and two volumes of theatre history; *A Brighter Sunshine* (polygon, 1983) and *Playing for Scotland* (Mercat Press, 1996) together with his cultural history of Edinburgh, published in the *Cities of the Imagination* series from Signal Books of Oxford (2001).

Formerly Writer-in-Residence to Lothian Schools (1974-77), Resident Playwright at the Royal Lyceum Theatre (1981-83), Fellow in Creative Writing at the University of Dundee (1987-89), William Soutar Fellow in Perth (1991-93) and Royal Literary Fund Fellow at Napier University (2000-01), Donald Campbell's stage drama has won three Scotsman "Fringe Firsts" for productions during the Edinburgh International Festival and his radio work has been recognized by international awards on three continents; *A Clydebuilt Man* (New York, 1983), *The Miller's Reel* (Sydney, 1987) and *The Year of The Bonnie Prince* (Monte Carlo, 1996).

www.ingramcontent.com/pod-product-compliance
Lightning Source LLC
Chambersburg PA
CBHW060805050426
42449CB00008B/1541